# commercial
# breaks

lisa rabey

To the men who've made love to me:
Chuck, Miguel, Alan, Matt, Chad, Andrew,
Mark, Danny, Mike, Jeff, Patrick,
Paul, Jon, Justin, and Thom.

And as always, to my brother Michael.

Love hard, love always, love to the end

# INTRODUCTION

I need to set the scene.

In the spring of 1996, I was an almost 24-year-old, newly diagnosed bipolar who had large social life online. In those days, chat was done via internet relay message (IRC) which was the precursor to AOL chat which was the precursor to Discord and Slack.

25 years on and we're still looking to make that human connection.

I became enthralled with IRC almost immediately as it allowed me to make connections to different people, cultures, and ideas worldwide. Holy shit! I'm talking to someone in France while I live in Michigan? MAGIC!

IRC fueled my mania to play out different scenarios living in my head. I could be anyone I wanted to be without judgment. It was, and still is, intoxicating.

I somehow found my way into a chat room called #easteden and between it and another channel or two, I met most of the people mentioned in these pieces.

(I met my husband on IRC in #philosophy the winter of 1996. To say IRC had an impact on me is an understatement.)

#

There are two pieces in this chapbook. The first is *Downpour On My Soul* written between April 20 – 22, 1996. Over those two days I wrote *Downpour on My Soul,* I was buoyed on cigarettes and Diet Coke. What I didn't know then was the jet propelled writing was actually mania exacerbated by the caffeine. I remember barely sleeping. I remember listening to the mix tapes I made. I remember drinking lots and lots of Diet Coke. I remember not wanting to go to class or head to work because I had important things to say.

25 years is a million miles away.

A year later, I wrote *Downpour Revisited* as a complement and follow up to *Downpour On My Soul. Downpour Revisited* has its own energy and it is structured differently. It doesn't read as a year-long follow up but as if someone else wrote it entirely.

I believe you can't have one without the other.

#

What are the pieces about? Good question. In the broad sense they are about love, relationships, and belonging. About feeling loved and wanted. Needed. Adored. Also confused. Hopeful and hopeless.

At 24, you think you know everything and half-hearted relationship attempts with high school boys, barely out of puberty, are your experiences with intimate love. The internet comes blazing into your life and suddenly guys who like you for you are everywhere. Tired of being objectified by those who attempt to woo you in person, meeting men on the internet allows you to find love where your mind is ultimately what's being objectified.

It's a pretty good set-up.

#

The very first internet relationship I had was with Matt who, god knows what channel I met him on, came to visit me in the fall of 1995. We broke up a few months later with his adage of, "I'm getting back together with my (local) girlfriend." So of course, my life ended and there would be no one else on the horizon.

We know how that story goes, don't we?

(Matt and I are friends on Facebook these days. I don't think either of us want to admit we're now older. Trivia: I am now friends with most of the men mentioned, romantic or otherwise, in this piece. Apparently, I am that memorable and we are all old.)

After Matt, relationships came and went, online and off. One would start, end, and another almost immediately began. Most were kept in the online world while a few would venture forth to meet in person.

. #

The reception of these pieces was interesting. I was pushing my voice out into the void where I used to think no one was listening, and now everyone was listening. Most loved it. Many thought I was a whore or an attention seeker. I received emails from people who could commiserate and emails from those who attempted to berate me for my "unattractive behavior" and then in the same breath ask me if I was up for phone or cam sex. The latter wanted me to be their dirty little secret. (Mostly staunch conservatives.)

The pieces also turned off many a would-be suitor as they didn't want to end up in the "annals of Lisa's life." Fair enough. Then I was angry for their slight but now, when I should understand reticence and privacy, I still feel their inability to jump head first is cowardly.

Some things never change.

From what I've also been able to cull from past lovers, the attraction to me was my fearlessness and tenacity to burn 1000x brighter than anyone they had ever met. I gave them all of me and in return, most could not make that leap to join me. With a few exceptions, most of these men left because I was "too much" only to come find me later to beg my forgiveness but I had moved on.

I always moved on. Someone out there had to understand and get me.

Now I know the burn was mostly mania but some of it was not. One of the things I adore about myself twenty-five years later is that my goal remains the same: to love someone as fiercely as I could ever love and to be loved as fiercely. (And the cheeky part of me says if they don't want or can't handle me – not only can they go fuck themselves but they are also not worthy.)

I'm still not afraid to take chances

The reactions were always passionate and I think at the core of it all, it sparked something from within for anyone who read it. Those same people were often likely afraid to admit just how much passion there was, at the time.

While everything changes, nothing changes.

Lisa Rabey

*Editor's note: The following has been cleaned up for clarity, spelling, and grammatical errors.*

# DOWNPOUR ON MY SOUL

## Station break
These images won't leave my mind

Pittsburgh

Standing in Chad's room. I am wearing his shorts, which are too big for me, they hang low on my hips. I lift my shirt to show him my freshly pierced naval. Ecstatic that I had finally done it, he leans forward and leaves kisses around the piercing. I stretch out and run my fingers through his long glorious hair. He looks up at me and tells me he loves me.

## Commercial 2
DeMoNBoX's friend came on channel today. When I ask politely how everyone is, he tells me Robert is back with is ex gf. The same one he left for me. Why does this NOT surprise me?

## Commercial 3
"One" is on the radio. JR and I are slow dancing to the song.

## Commercial 4
Matt has arrived in Grand Rapids

After many drinks, we are in the motel room. I am naked from the waist up. My skirt is barely covering my nether regions as I sit on Matt's lap. Dark eyes into dark eyes. He tells me he could be with me forever. He has never loved anyone like this.

## Commercial 5
Andrew

Glorious wonderful Andrew
He has asked me to marry him
Should I accept?
Simunye
"I will be the first. I want to be the first. I am first."
He says that I am the soul of his creations
Should I believe him?

## Commercial 6
I am rotating my navel ring

I hear creaking up the stairs
Parents are in bed
It's not my brother
I stand in the doorway, waiting to see who it is
I am not afraid
It's Nate, coming to get something for my brother.
Nate then proceeds to tell me my 7 foot brother is renegotiating to get back with his 5'3" girlfriend
They have been together for three years
Story of my life: Tall guys and short chicks

## Commercial 7
"How do u know Andrew is your soul mate?"

## Commercial 8
JR - discussion last summer
"I lied. I thought you were different. Then I left school and realized that there were people like me."
A phone call a few months later
It's JR
"I was wrong."

It's too late, I am with someone else now.

## Stop the tape

Chad - "You used me and you lied."

Matt - "Don't be so self-righteous."

Greg - "Why can't you pronounce Oregon?"

Mark - "I'm married and I have a gf."

JR- "I think a part of me fell in love."

Jeff - "Where have you been all my life?"

Andrew - "Love you lots darling!!"

## Another scene

Pittsburgh

Hair's wet and plastered to my scalp. My face is aglow and damp. I just made love to Chad in the shower. After sending him to bed. I trot downstairs to visit with Sass

Sitting with her on-line, Lee suddenly appears in #Easteden. I have not talked to him since I left school few weeks previously. I tell him I am in Pittsburgh, with Chad and Sass. I also tell him I had just made love to Chad

He gets jealous

Wants, in detail, how Chad makes love

"Does he have a big cock?" he asks

We go to war

Lee confesses he fell in love with me

I am what he dreamed of. My fault for being who I am today

I am confused

Sass leaves me alone

Lee wants me to fly to Seattle to be with him over my upcoming spring break

He wants to take care of me. He wants me to be naked at all times He whispers how he wants me to be his sexual slave, to be available for him at all times, regardless of where we are

Did I mention Lee has a BA in Philosophy, MA in English and is working on his Ph.D. in Metaphysics?

My face gets flush
My heart quickens
He says maybe one day we could be friends
I abruptly run upstairs
I strip my clothes off and crawl into bed with Chad
Chad turns around and grabs for me like he always does when we sleep
Curled up, spoon fashion, this 6'3, 220lb man holds me to his body like a doll
I kiss his forehead
He wakes up
We make love

## February 17th
I am no longer in contact with JR, Greg, Matt or Lee

Browsing on DalNet, I join the only populated channel
They ask for age/sex check
I hate that
Nevertheless, I type it in
23/Female
A most deranged man starts messaging me
RockRabbit
Andrew
We go to war
Holy shit!
He has a brain!
And he is 23/Male
He asks for a picture of me
I get one of him first
Wow! What a babe!
Wow! What a stud!
He demands I e-mail him
I take his address, blasé I might add
Next day, I get on DalNet

No e-mail from the Rabbit
I see him on the channel
I whois to verify
I wonder if he will message me?!
He does
When I message him back, his away notice says, "Waiting for the
babe!"

I chuckle
He gets angry! I gave him the wrong address!
No I didn't, I promise
I e-mail him to show him I didn't lie
I get bombarded with e-mail
We talk the whole day
Next day
I find him again

I start messaging him
No response
He's whooping it up on some channel
He told me he was SHY!
Fuck it
Next day, more e-mail
We meet again
No mention of the day before
We get cyber married that Thursday
War of emotion

War of feeling
He challenges
I challenge right back
Party Hardy!
Rock and Roll!
Drink a fifth!
Smoke a bowl!
Too many emotions

I say things

I question my ability to love
Do I love Andrew?
Do I mean what I say?
Yes, I do, I love Andrew

## My god!
I look at my watch

I have been writing straight for over 3 hours
My ashtray is full of butts
I count the pages

## My hair has completely dried
It's too thick

Ack!
Smoke keeps going up my nose
My hair hangs in my face, its natural wave making designs on the
paper
I can't SEE!
I push it behind my ears.

## March
I'm home from Texas

No, I don't want to talk about it
Chad is no longer IRCing
My fault
Matt and I become friends
He's living with the woman he left me for
Andrew speaks about coming here to be with me everyday

He wants me to meet Thys, his friend from DalNet
I meet Thys and his wife
Thys is from South Africa as well
He fell in love with an American Girl
After $10,000 in phone bills and nearly a year of talking on the net,
he moves to the States
Thys helps us with what I must do, what Andrew must do

Immigrations has gotten tighter
Andrew has to go home
It's late for him
Thys invites me to meet his wife. Ask her about what she went
through

"Oh! Your Rabbit's girl in NY! He's told us so much about you!"
"NY? No, I'm sorry, I'm in Michigan."
"Oh. Perhaps I have you two confused with another couple."

No, sorry… Thys said the same thing to me…

"No. Tell me how long have you known Andrew?"
"Well, (I lie), that is how long I've dated Andrew."
"Oh well…I could be mistaken."

Quickly, I think back. Andrew told me when he had been planning to
move here, to NY no less, when we first met
I ask Andrew directly
No comment
I e-mail him

He e-mails me back. Tells me he met a young woman last summer on
IRC. Never been more than friends. She helped him out with his
depression
Hmmm…something is not jelling here

Now he tells me he last spoke to her in November. We met in
February. Thys says he first met Andrew in January. But yet he and
his wife knew about Andrew's "girl in NY." Yet Andrew tells me she
is somewhere in England

Does this make sense?
I don't mention it anymore
He seems genuinely upset

## Chad! Chad! Chad!
God damn you to every living hell

Emotionally exhausting me
The day before I leave for Texas, he tells me he loves me so much it hurts

He wants to go kill himself. I grow tired of his behavior, I try to ignore him

I can't. We talk. He tells me he loves me so much. Wanted to call me before I left

No, no no Chad

"I know what you are doing, you are trying to make me hate you…I cant. I love you, beautiful."

Oh god…my heart rips in two
I meet Andrew, break it off with Chad, and am going to Texas to meet Robert

I should be hung

Texas
Best to block it out of mind

All I can remember is walking into Austin International crying
I was going home

Yawn
4 hours of writing

I can't stop
Gotta keep going

A Dino Pez dispenser is in front of me
Bought as a peace offering for Chad

Never sent it
The candy still sits in my drawer

Find out Sandy is going to go see Chad.
Goddamn him!

He is yelling at me about Andrew
And here he has been talking to Sandy the whole time
He says you got to understand, she was there when we were fighting
Besides you have Andrew

Or do I?

Friday, April 19
Andrew surprises me with a new animation design for my homepage.

Elated, I tack it up all over the place
He needs to talk to me, will do it via e-mail
Matt shows up
Andrew then tells us the news he was going to e-mail me with
Andrew got the job

Matt breaks out the virtual champagne
I ask for a beer
Andrew a Coke
I propose a toast
Matt says there better be tears in Andrew's eyes after that toast
Andrew is a lucky man
Andrew points to a tear in his eyes

*Glycerine* is on
Reminds me of Chad at his apartment in Pittsburgh

We are lying in his bed
Naked
He is so shy about his body
It's late at night. We are snuggling together
The radio is on, *Glycerin* comes on. We are giggling like mad children
Legs interlaced

He's holding me tight

His bed is so small. The Pooh bear I gave him is on the floor
We sleep like that all night
I wake him up like that, making love to him

"Mmmm…I love you baby." he says

# A piece of my hair falls from my ponytail
It falls down the front of my face

Its tip tickling my lips
I haven't been kissed in a long time

# After Andrew's received the news of the record contract
I am elated

He told me earlier the news was good for me
I asked him more about the job
The bad news comes
He has to go to Jo'berg for the job
A month
He will not have IRC access
He can't or won't be able to talk to me, except maybe e-mail
I panic
I ask him if he will see his friend Val, who he met on IRC, while he is
there

Again no comment

"Lisa, you must understand. This will bring me the money I need to
get there.
I told you I'd follow you to the ends of the earth. That is my
decision. I
love you. I'm doing this for you. Everything I do, I do for you."

# Blast from the past
I am 19

A man I had met when I was 17 and dated on and off re-enters my
life

We had last parted on bad terms
Friends tell me he is in Guam
I get the number
I call

His roommates answer
When I leave my name and number, the roommate asks me if I was
"the" Lisa
He knew who I was!

Seems Miguel spoke about nothing but me
Miguel calls me back
We talk for hours
We conclude we are in love
He is working on bringing me to Guam
I call one night
He is drunk

He proceeds to tell me he has just made love to a 40 year old woman
He knew, I had, at that time, relatively little sexual experience. Not
the sex
goddess I am today

"Everything I do, I do for you baby."

Two weeks later, I meet Alan
Through a network of friends, Miguel finds out
Flies to GR from Guam, with a return ticket for me
I stay in GR

Excerpts from Jars of Clay's song, *Flood*
*Rain rain on my face / It's been raining, raining for days / My world is a flood / Slowly I become one with the mud / Lift me up when I'm falling / Lift me up / We can dive in / Lift me up I need you to hold me / Lift me up Keep me from drowning again*

You are my brown eyed girl!
Do you remember when, we used to sing:

sha de lallalallallallalalalalala ti da
sha de lallalallallallalalalalala ti da
sha de lallalallallallalalalalala ti da

OI!

It's late. 1:30am.
I've been writing nonstop for 5hrs

I am emotionally and physically tired
This must get done, tonight, for it's going on the web tomorrow
My brother walks in
I look at him
Black stuff is under his eyes
I peer closer
The boy is wearing makeup, including lipstick
Theresa, the 5'3" girlfriend, had done that

*Aeroplane* by the Chili Peppers
First heard it in Pittsburgh

Chili's the restaurant.
Chad and I went there after I got my navel pierced
Did you take Sandy there Chad?
Don't tell me. I don't want to know
Chad and I fed each other
I was in the bathroom cleaning my navel ring, a woman walked in
Saw what I was doing , turned around and left
Chad and I were there for awhile

Chad was yelling at me because I was so stubborn on seating. I
wanted smoking section. Chad said he didn't care. We waited for 1/2
hour plus. For a table on Sunday night while others went ahead of us.
I was convinced it was because the little fluff chick was eyeing him

She was all of 17

"All the women want me"

Yeah Chad, I know

Even as a joke, I knew it was true. We'd go out, I'd watch the women watch him. I asked him if he thought of other women. "Guy stuff" he called it

I laughed

Friends would tell me he would get on really late at night and talk about me, how much he loved me. How beautiful I was. How much he loved me

He was always drunk when he did that

Anonymous quote from an anonymous source
"A Chad in Pittsburgh is worth 2 Andrews in Pretoria."

My cat Chester just walked in
Biohazard once asked me if anyone had ever told me how feline I was. No I replied.

He said think about it, you use words and gestures, like frisky and purring. My movements are similar as well. My mood is like a cat, very picky and very independent

I asked for but never received a collar
The idea of being petted appeals to me

Am I finally running out of thoughts?
NEVER!

Gotta keep writing and revising.

Two pictures of Andrew are taped to my computer at the Collegiate
Someone keeps stealing them

Ha!

I have more

The staff, particularly Les, is convinced I am copying the photos from a magazine

No, sorry guys, I really know him
Heather reads a few of the letters Andrew has sent me, to prove he exists

"Wow! He really loves you Lisa!"

"Yeah, I like to think so."

"But I don't believe he's coming here. I'm not saying that because you can't get a guy like Andrew, but it's just that …..he's gorgeous!"

Wonderful ditzy Heather! I love ya, but fuck you

## A recent letter from one of my oldest friends, Shelly
"I'm glad to hear that you have found a new man(Chad)! But shy…that doesn't sound like your style! Well, I guess it would counteract with your outrageousness so that you would go good together!"

Fuck, I need to write to her more often

## Andrew and I got into our first fight
A serious fight a few weeks ago, over a stupid package. Since we had meet, he started putting a package together for me. Elated, I did the same. and shipped it off. I told him 8-10 days at the most. He received it in 10 days after I sent it. It is now April, the package he promised to send in February is not here. We argued heavily.

"I goddamn love you Lisa!"

"I want this package to be the greatest thing you have ever received. I want it to be birthday, Christmas, everything rolled up into one."

He sent the package on April 4th.

17 days later it is still not here.

## My friend Jen
(Ed in chief of the *Collegiate*) and I went to a bar called Jimmy's.
While walking through the crowded bar, I stood tall. 6'1 in my boots.
I dwarfed over 99% of the females and 50% of the males.

As I go get our drinks, two guys are in front of me, dressed preppie. I
hate preppie guys. The one in front looks behind his friend and into
my eyes. He whispers to his buddy, "Look at that babe behind you.
She's hot!"

## Andrew just told me how much he loves me.
Seems now that word of him having a girlfriend is out, and he is
dating again, all the women are calling him

He says I'm the reason he doesn't go out on the weekends
He doesn't want to break their hearts; he's too loyal to me
I think my heart broke a little more.
I miss him so much

## Sherry says I'm intimidating to men.
She says it's because I'm too smart or too intelligent. Jen (ed in chief)
says I look like I have always something to prove.

Perhaps

## November 1995
Washington DC

Jen (ed in chief) and I get all dressed up to go out to dinner. I'm
uncomfortable in a skirt. I hate skirts. Jen says I look fabulous.
Walking arm-in-arm down Connecticut Ave., we are dressed to kill.
We are both wearing black leather jackets, my darkness contrasting
with her blondness. Our short skirts showing off our long legs.
Guys are driving by, hollering and whistling.

Jen and I laugh.

I've been writing for six straight hours. Its now 2:30am.
I calculate the time difference where everyone is at 8:30am for
Andrew. Morning, darling

A kiss?
Hehehe…go brush your teeth darling
2:30am for Matt, Chad, Jeff and Mark

Night guys
Let me tuck you in

Okay, Okay Mark, I will let your wife tuck you in
Here's Pooh, Chad. Don't rip his head off please
Here's Sebastian the bunny, Andrew, take good care of him please
11:30pm for Greg. I know you are having fun, don't do what I
wouldn't do!

*wink*

## The mighty KC
Hey Chad!

Yeah, you!

Remember we were driving to Sass's, this song came on. You
covered my eyes to shield me from Taco Bell and giggled about it
later?

## 21 pages
I don't think I will get all of this on the web tomorrow unless I type
really fast

## Matt and I got into an argument while we were dating
He said not everyone wants what I have

Ohh, but you're wrong Matt

Recall when my so-called friends laughed at the idea of you and I
getting together?

When they saw you, they went after you with a vengeance

## You and I had gone to a club with Sherry and Rick
I remember what I was wearing. A pair of blue jeans and a
formfitting cream-
colored short-sleeved turtleneck

We had spent NINE hours at the mall. (Word of caution, I do not
like the mall)
We got fairly drunk

I would go dancing while you watched
Oh yeah baby, I'm different
I don't bump and grind to the music
I make love to it
I have been raving for a few years now
Other people move out of the way for me

You just watched, Jack and Coke in hand
My father is an alcoholic
That night you smelled like my father
Later on I asked you to slow dance with me. You would not
You later walked up to me, and started feeling on my ass
Moving your hands up my body
I was talking to a guy friend. You got jealous
You turned me around, running your hands up and down my body
From my crotch, over my stomach, feeling on my breasts
We didn't care
People were watching

Later I had helped you into bed
200-pound man I got undressed
You wanted your boxers
You cried for your boxers
I struggled and got them on you
I took care of you that night
While on the phone with Sherry, I alternated between getting things
for you and smoking a cigarette

You almost cried
You said that no one treated you that wonderfully before
While gossiping with Sherry, you kept talking
"I can hear you, you know!"
"Shut up Matt. Go to bed!"

Men are like children

## I just got the weirdest reaction to this page so far
I had given Chad the URL. I wanted him to know why I do the things I do

I did not expect a response from him
I did not expect anything from him
I asked him if he read it when he got on-line, he said no. I said please, you don't have to tell me
He said maybe
I said look, if you read it or not, fine, you don't have to tell me
He didn't say anything.
Then he told me he read it
He was so ANGRY at me!
Calling it slander!
Getting all fired up about it
Look Chad, punish me if you want to, but not till you read the rest of the story!

## I had never been kissed on New Year's Eve
I was damned and determined I was going to be kissed

Never having seen Chad before I met him, I had no idea what to expect
When I saw him, my mouth dropped open
He just radiated sensuality from his long hair to his full lips
Nervous, I walked in. He was working on installing a modem
Hank and I helped
Up the narrow stairs we climbed
He refused to look at me
I wondered if he didn't like me

I was wrong

My one night stay turned into five days

At Sass's party, people were giggling about us
We had gotten lost on our way to Sass's
A normal one hour drive took us three hours. Rumors flew around it
was due to either

## I gave him head on the way down OR
We stopped to make love

## It was neither
I freaked while driving. We had gotten lost. Chad held my hand the
whole way while telling me to stop singing. He often commented on
how for someone with a voice like mine, I still couldn't carry a tune.

My heart problem had started getting worse. I ran upstairs to get my
meds. I had forgotten to take them while I was at Chad's. Ripping
apart my bags, I found my pills. Once I ripped the cap off, the pills
went flying around the room

Chad sat me down on the bed and picked up all my pills off the floor

He sat and held me till the pain went away

## Getting ready for said party
Chad walked in while I was putting on makeup, something I rarely
do, Chad looked at me.

"You're too beautiful for makeup, you don't need it."

Sweet Chad
He loved me so much.

## Chad loved me so much that after I left Pitt the first time,
his previous interest called and phone sexed him

Chad loved me so much I heard rumors about him wanting Bridget's

sister
She thought he was hot.

But what does a 17 year old girl compare to a 23 year old woman?
I knew whose bed he'd be in
But the flirtation lasted after I left

3:30am
I am emotionally exhausted
So darling Andrew, dear Andrew
You have toyed with me
Teasing me about Val
Telling me when she's on the phone knowing....

Chad grabbed me and kissed me at the stroke of 12
This is going to be the best year of my life

You destroyed my trust Chad
I loved you so much

Alan and I were on our way to Jen's house
Zipping along the highway, I asked him if he had ever thought of kissing another woman.

For you see, I had thought about kissing another man
That bothered me. I loved Alan
I was confused
How could I be so in love with Alan and yet want to kiss this guy?

Alan replied "I thought about fucking Todd's girlfriend."
Todd's girlfriend (whose name I can not remember) was tall, blonde and perfect
Aghast, I stayed silent

Jen said I was being stupid
Alan loved me so where was the problem?

Some months later, Todd's gf walked into a store where I

worked
We started talking

The night Morrissey made a surprise appearance in Grand Rapids,
Alan had wanted me to go, but I had to work

Seems since Todd and his girlfriend had broken up for that day
Alan asked her out

Alan and I were still together
When Alan showed up later, I asked him about it
He changed his story five different times

I sighed

## Mark wanted me to talk about him
Yeah Mark, I do love you

But I'm never ever leaving Andrew, he deserves my respect, my
loyalty and all of my love
Mark told me he wished things could have been different

It's gone too far

You will always be my friend, Mark, I just can not love you like you
want to be loved
You know I love Andrew

I can't give him up
I can't ask you to give up your life for me either
It's unfair to your spouse

Andrew is free
Andrew accepts me
No matter how I hurt to get to the truth
Andrew is what I have been waiting for all of my life

For you see, Mark, I could not have written this without an Andrew
in my life

He is the one that pushed me to do this, to air my laundry
No one has ever done that to me before
Andrew is my life!

## Three days after Christmas 1992
Alan breaks up with me

I am an emotional wreck

At a New Year's Eve party
I drink too much
I get too high
I pass out

Alan calls, asking about me

Few days later we go on a date
Sitting at the corner of Brooklyn and 28th
He looks at me, I look at him
We start to kiss
After dinner we go back to my house

We make love

## April 1993
I'm sitting at home

Jen is now living with me and working where I work
I am her boss
She calls on the phone
"There is a problem, you need to get down here."

I drive all two blocks
She sits me down
"How are you and Alan?" she asks

"We still fuck if that is what you mean."
"He's seeing another woman," she states

I look at her
"For awhile now, at least six months."
We have only been apart for four

I call Alan's house
No, he is not home
I walk outside and jump on the hood of the car he bought me
I jump up and down on the hood
I walk up and down the length

## Mid-April 1993
I go to see the JudyBats

Julie, Fernando and I go
Fueled by my adrenaline, Fernando and I rave hard during the sets of
the show

Alan watches me from the corner
We talk

He asks who Fernando is
"Julie's man," I reply

Where is "vicegrips" I ask
At work

That night, I am asleep
Spring air is coming through the window

I feel a hand on my arm
It's Alan
We go downstairs
We make love all night

It would be one of the last times I would ever see him

"Ohh Lisa, I love you so much!"

## Sometime around my birthday, 1993

I'm drunk on the couch

It's 3am
The phone rings
"Hi, I just wanted…."

It's Alan

"Where are you?"
"Michelle's"

*click*
*RING*

"What?"
"Lisa…."
"Look Alan, you stay on your side of town and I will stay on my side."

*click*

Early June, 1993
I'm at work

The phone rings
"Where were you last night?"

It's Alan

"I was at Scotts."
"Who the hell is Scott?"
"Why do you care? You're marrying Michelle."

"I love you Lisa"
"She's not you"

Mid-June, 1993
"I need to see you"

It's Alan

"Please" he begs
He comes over
"You've never looked more beautiful to me."

I had worked 14 straight hours
It is 12pm

The sun is shining into my front living room
We make love

## Late June/Early July, 1993
I am at a local nightclub, Dick's Resort

"Alternative night"

First time I had ever been there
I am dancing up a storm
Drinks are being bought for me

I look up
See Alan and Michelle walk in the door
Alan walks around the club, watching me

My friend Jamie says he wants to talk to me
We go to the side
We start arguing

Michelle walks up
I tell her to fuck off
She and I start arguing

I say fuck it
She says my car, all $6000 of it, is a piece of shit

I say hey, that is okay
My car will outlast the plastic and glass ring he bought you

The car cost 6K
The ring 500 dollars

She calls me a slut
I throw my drink to the side

I wrap my fingers around her throat
Took Alan and two bouncers to pull me off of her

All I kept hearing as I walked outside was
"I've got the ring"

I never saw Alan again

Earlier this year
I ran into some friends of Alan's and mine when we were together

Alan really did marry her
They have a child

All of the friends we hung out with and had gotten married when we
met
Are now divorced

I walk away
I shudder

Earlier Sunday, sitting in the lab
I was talking to Troy

I looked up and see a guy I dated very briefly during the "Alan"
trauma
I slept with him
It took me till today to remember his name

I'm sitting at Kalamazoo college gym
Watching the AAU team play ball

Shirts against skin

commercial breaks

I watch while I write

Sweat pours down their backs
They are all tall
Some have better bodies then most
Some are good-looking, others are not

I wonder what it would be like to make love to a man
Not a boy
A man

Sascha says she is always looking out for cheap and easy guys
I wonder if I am cheap and easy

No, I conclude
I am not

## My IRC friend Bryan
keeps telling me he loves me more then Andrew ever would

I don't think he knows just what he is saying
Bryan is 19

## When I was a little girl
I wanted to remain a virgin till I was married

Friends teased me
When I was 17, I met Scott
We slept together three days later

*smack*

"You are not wearing that outfit"
"But Scott…"
"Change….NOW!!"

## Sitting at Magoo's with Sherry and Matt
Sherry says, "Oh shit!"

I look at her
She mouths the words "Miguel"
I turn and look
Miguel is looking at me, my arm is around Matt
He turns and walks away

Matt asks who that was
I tell him
He points to some small icky looking blonde
"She looks just like…" his last serious girlfriend

## Mid-December 1995
"Matt I have to tell you something"

"Mmmm..what?"
"I'm seeing someone and I wanted to tell you before you heard it
from someone else"
"Oh, I'm so glad! For you see Lisa, I'm seeing someone else too!"

I prattle on about Chad
Chad is so incredible

"Who is it, Matt?"
"Janice"
Janice, the woman he lived with over the summer

"You have nothing to worry about Lisa. She's nothing compared to
you."
They are now living together

## So you see Andrew,
I told you this is not because I don't love you but because I do. I
tried to explain to you the basis of IRC relationships. They're intense,
surreal and fast paced

I am now emotionally exhausted

I can no longer fight

You explained to me that to love someone else is impossible

Perhaps you are different, perhaps the truths not jelling are all misunderstandings. I am not perfect I know this. I am merely human After this weekend bout of soul searching, if something happened to you while you are in Jo'berg, I would not be surprised.

I've concluded there is something about me, not the men in my life, regardless if it's IRC or real life, that has caused the things that have happened to be

I have a special talent for picking up on emotionally crippled guys. I give them something no woman has given them or will ever give them again. I accept them for themselves, nothing more, nothing less. I give them 200%. But I am a tough mistress

I demand a lot
They will leave me experiencing something they will never have again
But they love me so much, they have to leave me

Find someone more realistic
Someone not a dreamer

The idea of me is more appealing then the real me
Something I have always known
Something I have always accepted
I know that I am "too much"

When the going gets rough, the rough gets going
So Andrew, you have your groupies who don't know you
Your female friends
Val, who is but three hours from you and whom you talk with
And ask yourself, will they love you and accept you like I do?

Come or go, stay or leave, I'm emotionally dead
I cannot compete any longer

I refuse to compete
I am ME!

You say my soul is pure, my heart is pure. You say I am what you
have waited for all your life
You may think I am being silly

You may say that what you have told me about yourself should prove
beyond a reasonable doubt that I am all you need
True

Here is where my dual nature comes in
I am skeptical, but I am also trusting
Perhaps that is why I dig surrealism
It shows me anything is possible

Why I believe in romance
Why I always crave the impossible

Why I always look for the best
Why I write

So Andrew
Here I am
Love me or hate me
Say you know me or you don't

Every man that I have ever dated seriously or has liked me
a lot, says the man I am going to marry is a lucky guy

I am special
I am different
I am not like the rest

So then why

     a.   I am still single in real life?
     b.   Do they always break up with me?

Driving home from K-Zoo
My brother and I are talking

I ask him if I am cool
For being an older sister
He says no
I start to laugh
I ask why
He says because I don't go chill with friends, drink or go out
anymore

I stay in my room and write all night
I am too intelligent
When friends come over to our house, and we start dogging on each
other, it's about stuff no one has a clue about
He says when I make a cut against someone, they don't understand

I laughed

That's me
Too intelligent

I watch
I write
I happen to know things others don't
I am the queen of useless information

Spring has sprung!
I love spring

I always feel reborn
I crave sun
I come out of my shell

Call my friends
"Hey guys!"
"I'm HERE!!!"
They all expect it of me

Lisa hibernates during the winter

Comes out fighting in the spring

## Pearl Jam
Chad looks like Eddie Vedder

He would mock every song that came on the radio
I would start to laugh

## One night Chad picked me up
Put me on his dresser

We tried to make love
It didn't work

## Chad is so far my favorite person to make love to
I would wash his hair

I would scrub him down from head to toe
I would zerbert his belly
He would laugh

One particular time, we got a little carried away
We left the shower running
I put the seat down on the toilet
I sat him down

I got on and rode him
Hard
Kissing him to stifle his cries
I slowly pulled off of him

Got on my knees and performed fellatio
I swallowed
He watched the whole time
I kissed him
We finished our shower

Sass always teased us
Out loud questioning why the bathroom was always so soaked

We'd giggle

## When Chad and I were arguing
He asked me to tell him everything

I told him about Andrew
My soul mate

He cried
My heart broke in two
I told Andrew

Andrew understood. Told me because I had been with Chad, it was more than real to me. That he could understand

He knew I still loved Chad
Too many demons in Chad's past
I could not help him
I could barely help myself
I walked away from Chad

It was one of the hardest things I ever had to do

## My brother just walked in
"Writing another book?"

Night Jeff

## Blunt sexuality has always bothered me
I watch these fluff chicks show everything off

I laugh at them
Sex to me is mysterious
Why I prefer boxers to briefs
I want to use my mind to imagine the package
I want to imagine what it's like underneath the jeans and T-shirts

I like being discreet in my clothing
Show a bit of leg

Wear a form-fitting shirt

## Andrew and I do not discuss sex
It's frustrating

Sometimes I want him to make love to me
I want to imagine what it would be like
The very first time we tried I could see it all
Clearly in my mind
Scared the living hell out of me
It was that real to me
He left abruptly
Apologized profusely the next day
I said it was all right

## Sometimes when Andrew describes how he would kiss me
It scares me

It's too real
I can feel my mouth drop, I can feel the heat from his skin, and I can
feel his breath against my face
Then he leaves
I find some schmuck on-line
I abuse him sexually to get rid of my frustration
I never tell Andrew
He says he does not want to know
It would break his heart

So I don't tell him

*If I had a million dollars / I would buy you a house / If I had a million dollars
/ I would buy furniture for your house / If I had a million dollars / I would buy
your love*

## Andrew's told me he hates himself for loving me
He swore he would never love again

Then he met me
He pushes and probes

Leaving me wanting more

He gave me himself!
Then he took it away
He's so angry
So frustrated

Paints me pretty pictures
Writes me poems
But no more

## I have a plethora of Andrew pictures
He looks so beautiful to me

Some are modeling pics
Others are self done compilations
My favorite one is one he put together
Blue eyes looking directly at you
A Mona Lisa smile

ANDREW!
I told you NO EYES!
You lied to me!

## Can't make it real
Can't make it real

Don't make it real
Don't make it real
Don't tell me you love me

*If you save yourself / you will make him happy*

Does love exist?

Yes
No
Stay-go
Love me-hate me

worship me-condemn me
emotions
feelings
Too much it hurts

"I have told a lie"
"I have not been true"
"Do not cry"

*If you fool yourself, you will make him happy*

**L** – *is for LOVE baby*
*O* – *is for ONLY you that I do*
*V* – *is for loving VIRTUALLY everything that you are*
*E* – *is for loving almost EVERYTHING that you do*
*R* – *is for RAPE me*
*M* – *is for MURDER me*
*A* – *is for ANSWERING all of my prayers*
*N* – *is KNOWING your loverman's going to be the answer to all yours*

Words said
Promises broken

So that is me
Sunday April 21, 1996 11:45pm
My room is a pigsty
My mouth feels like a party happened and I wasn't invited
I drank too much Diet Coke
I smoke too much
Sometimes….

*Somebody told me, this is the place / Where everything is better / Everything is safe…*

*1/2 hour later, we packed up our things*
*Said we send letters*
*And all of those little things*
*They knew we were lying*

*They smiled just the same*
*They seemed to have forgotten*
*We already came*
*People don't know you*
*Trust is a joke*

"She likes to look for things that she'll never find"

A few days ago, a bunch of us were on-line
#Easteden

I say hi to Chad
HI CHADIUS!
We are becoming friends again
I think
We have a topic war
Chad puts in something about a 747
747 is the name we gave my vibrator
I start giggling
Chad and I giggle on line
I could see him sitting at his desk
Stroking his goatee
giggling
Sandy was on-line
I do not think she had a clue to what we were talking about

A few anonymous sources told me recently
That Sandy is not sure if Chad likes her

He still has a love/hate relationship with me. She knows this. He
doesn't talk about me. But people know
They can see the tension when the three of us are on-line

When Sandy came back from Pitt
Everyone was dying to know what happened

But no one would ask
I have balls
I asked

"Chad is so adorable"
Stupid bitch!
Chad is not adorable
He is a child in a man's body!
He radiates 100% pure sex!
I wanted to smack her

"Did you get to wash his hair?"
"Oh yes!"
I concluded they had sex
No one knows for sure
Some things are better left unsaid

I can talk to Matt about his sex life
For some reason he has lost his passion

Matt's a good guy
Just needs to loosen up
I am a free person
It would not have worked
He fucked up
Life goes on

The night of the party at Sass's
Chad and I are lying naked in bed

We try to be quiet
We hear Sass and her man going at it
The headboard bangs against the wall
Love cries are loud
Chad and I start giggling
Our giggling gets louder

A male voice yells out
"Quit playing with your sister!"
We yell, "Night Mom and Dad!"

We are laughing so hard, we start crying
Chad slips out of bed to lock the door

The moonlight streams across his body
I look at him
He looked so incredible to me

## The final time I saw Chad
We're sitting in his room

I am sitting at an odd angle
My navel hurts because of the piercing
I'm talking on-line to Lilly
She asks me to fwap him
And as I turn to do so
I look at him. He's leaning on his bed
He's wearing his blue cardigan
It's so cold in his apartment
His hair is behind his ears
He looks at me, mouths "I love you"
He smiles as he does his homework
"Why the hell do I need to know this?"
I laugh

## When Sandy got back from Pitt
She said she was glad to be sleeping in her own bed

When I left Pitt, I cried!
Chad was like a huge furnace
He'd hold me all night
Sometimes he'd wake me
Sometimes I'd wake him

## The final night Chad and I were together
We didn't make love

My tummy hurt too much

We talked all night
Trying hard to not sleep
But I had to go home
Chad had school

I barely slept that night
I just watched him
Conscious of the hours ticking by
When the alarm went off, he woke me
Chad is NOT a morning person
As I go, I watch him watch me
He e-mailed me later on
He ran out to kiss me good-bye
I was already gone
He was so upset, he stayed home and slept with Pooh

Yeah Andrew knows
He knows what I am

He's got his groupies
They all want him
He's a demi-god
He knows
Each move feels calculated
He tries to get me to show emotion
And so I do
You wanna hear me say it?
All right I will!

Yeah, I am jealous as hell, Andrew
I'm jealous of the women you've been with
I'm jealous of the lips you've kissed
I'm jealous of the bodies you've probed
I'm jealous as hell!!
I'm jealous of Val…you get to talk to her
Anytime you want!
I've got to live with four words

"Love you lots darling!"
I got jealous when you told me
"Desert, beer flowing, horny girls and one tall guy!"
It's not goddamn fair!
Yeah Andrew, that is why I netsex you!

You deprive me of tender touches and kisses
You make me beg for it
You never approach me
I'm always the aggressor
So I netsex you
Make you realize I am there
I describe actions
Drive your mind into overtime
Make you see my body as I often saw yours in my dreams
That's how I fight

With sex
Childish

No one ever said I played fair
You know you got me Andrew
Because you've never given me what the one thing I want/need from you!
You gloat!
You know you do

'Cause just when I think I've got you, you say "talk time"
And I've got to shift gears
I'm rearing to go
you tell me to stop!

ARGHHHHHHHHHH!!!!!!

I'm not stupid Andrew
You pour all your emotions, your passion into your letters, your pictures
But lately I've got nothing from you

And so you wonder
Why I cling
Why I question when you say you are going away
Why when you say yes, I still want to marry you
That loving someone other then me is impossible
That you never, ever want to break up

That I don't feel reassured
Why I question if you are tired of fighting me
If you've given up
On me
On us

## I can't break away

*All my life, I've wanted to fly*

*Like the birds you see way up in the sky / Making circles in the morning sun / Flying high in the sky / Till the day is done / I can't break away / Like a child in his fantasy / Punching holes in the walls of reality / All my life, I've wanted to fly / But I don't have the wings / And I wonder why / Oh well, mom told me when I was young / Stand tall girl, your number one / You can be what you want to be / But you can't shake the course of your destiny / I can't break away / One is one, two is two / You want me and I have you / I can't break away / No, no, no, no , no , no / I can't break away / Oh well, mom told me when I was young / Stand tall girl, your number one / You can be what you want to be / But you can't shake the course of your destiny / I can't break away/ /No. no. no. no, no / I can't break away / I can't break away / I can't break away / I CANT BREAK AWAY*

## Good night folks
This is it

Last one out, turn the lights off and lock the door

Started Saturday April 20th at 8:30pm
Finished Monday April 22nd at 1:40am

47 hand written pages
This is your life Lisa Marie-Louise Rabey
Permission not received for lyrics reprinted
Fuck the laws. Sue my ass. I don't have a pot to piss in anyway

## Night Andrew
No matter what happens after you read this, I love you, need you and want you. You are still my soul mate

Night Chad. I love you too. Please don't hate me for what I've done
Night Matt. Find someone you can love and trust. Be happy
Night Mark. Yeah, I love you too. But work things out in your life
Night Greg. Yeah (Ha!) I love you too. Another time, another place
Night Alan. You shaped my future, I don't hate you anymore. But I
hope you carry the guilt for the rest of your life
Night Miguel. You left me with a $1000 cell bill. I hope your past
catches up with you
Night Chuck. You broke my hear at 15. I hope one day you will be
free. I still wish you were my first
Night Scott. You were my first. I'm glad your life sucks
Night Josh. My best friend, companion in trouble and confidant. I
have not talked to you in six months. I hope you're happy
Night JR. You will always be my Henry to your Anais
Night Lee. Could have been, should have been, isn't
Night Jeff. I'm too corrupt for you. Find a pure woman

Night to all that I missed.

## The past is put to rest
The circle is finally complete

I'm free now
Free to fly
I exist
I am human
I no longer hate
And I have won

Curtain closes
Place darkens
The only sound heard is the flapping of film against the reel

# DOWNPOUR REVISITED

And so it begins again.

Another smoked filled night, with Sarah on the CD player, wondering what the hell is going on with my life.

And yes dear folks, those who have read my "stuffs" and emailed me, it's all true. Every spunky inch of it, dammit. I mean, who else but MOI can have a life such as this? I mean, hell, it's better then Melrose or 90210, but then again, I don't wear a size 2 or have an unlimited allowance.

I don't know why the caged bird sings.
I don't know why I fall in love.
I don't know why the earth is round.

*Under a blackened sky, far beyond the glaring street lights, sleeping on empty dreams...the vultures lie in wait. / You lay down beside me there, you were there with me every waking hour / So close I could feel your breath / When all we wanted was to dream, to have and to hold these precious little things... like every generation yields the new born hope unjaded by their years / Pressed up against the glass, I found myself wanting sympathy but to be consumed again / Oh I know would be the death of me / FOR THERE IS A LOVE THAT IS INHERENTLY GIVEN! / A kind of blindness offered to deceive and in that light of forbidden joy / Oh I know I wouldn't receive it / When all we wanted was to dream, to have and to hold that precious little thing / Like every generation yields the newborn hope unjaded by their years / You know if I leave you now, it doesn't mean I love you any less / It's just the state I'm in / I can't be good to anyone else like this / When all we wanted was to dream, to have and to hold that precious little thing / Like every generation yields the newborn hope unjaded by their years...* -- *Wait* by Sarah McLachlan

Don, I don't know
I always thought the answer to life's questions was "42," BUT I DON'T KNOW!
"Oh yeah?"
Yeah.
Dammit.

Don asked me if I ever read any of my stuff, (*I looked into your eyes, / they told me plenty*) and I said, "Yeah, but I can't keep reading it, it's like, thinking "that chick is weird!". (*I never thought you would stray / I thought I would be with you till my dying day*)

Not weird, just, I can feel her *pain*.
(*I used to think my life, was often empty*)

I'm stealing lyrics, because I can't comprehend what it is I want to say.
I have a lot to say dammit, but the words are not coming out the way that they should (*there was a freedom*).
So I just re-read (*I couldn't ever believe that you would might stray*).
Circles.
The answer to life's great mysteries are circles.

Okay, for those who don't know, Michael dumped me. He said "See ya later toots," kicked me to the curb, took the garbage out, "It just doesn't feel right." (You seemed so real to me). AFTER ALL THE BULLSHIT, ITS REFRESHING TO SEE!

Lies.
All Lies.

(*Don't tell me I haven't been good for you / Don't tell me I haven't been there for you / Don't tell me that nothing is good enough*)

Yeah, well, I got smart

Because YOU were the one who promised 12 millennium and all that jazz, when all I wanted was no.
(I didn't expect I would deserve so much more than this)
Just don't tell me why, because maybe I don't want to know.

   *sigh*

So, I read (and I can plug my own shit thankuverymuch), and it's like, you know, I can relate to that, HELL I WROTE IT!

Yeah, too much, that's me, in a nutshell.

In the past 22 months, I have roughly dated 15 guys, take or give a few.
And slept with about, erm, well, enough.

And it's like, I preach about TRUTH, and HONESTY, and what the hell, am *I* doing preaching about this bullshit?
(*Take her hand, she will lead you through the fire / and give you back hope / and hope that you won't take to much / she held us in our arms* "and it felt good")

And sometimes, (*I believe there is a distance I have wandered / Ohhh holding out / holding in / I believe this is heaven to no one else but me / And I will defend it as long as I can be left here to linger in silence*), at night, I can feel his pain. I can feel his (*I'm drunk in my desire / But I love the way you smile at me / the way your hands reach out / I believe*) pain (*This is heaven to no one else but me and I will defend it as long as I can be*) calling out to me, and it's like, I can't, I can't, I CAN'T.

(*It might not be right for you, but its right for me / I believe*)

I miss him.

And times like this, when I can almost hear him (well, with the marvels of modern technology, I have his voice recorded on .wavs "All because you wanted to hear my voice.")

(*There are two of us talking in circles, and one of us wants to leave*)

Cheap thrills.
But I miss him.

Are you reading this Michael? HMMMMM? (*What kind of love is this that's keep me hanging / I know to many people unhappy*). Well, good, pull up a seat, bring TheGnome and Sprite with you. Its going to be a trip worse than you have ever taken.

(*Your angels speak with gilded tongues*)
(*Hold on / hold on to yourself / for this is going to hurt like hell /*

*OHH GOD THE MAN I LOVE IS LEAVING! /*
*Am I heaven hero, am I in hell?*
*You will be strong tomorrow.*)

Are you sleeping peacefully, Michael?
Do you regret your decision?

And I remember the smile, I brought across his face, (*Your love is better than ice cream / better than anything else I could try / your love is better than ice cream / everyone here knows how to cry / it's a long way down / it's a long way down / it's along way down...to the place where we started / from / mmmmhmmmm / Your love is better than chocolate / better than anything I would try / ohh love is better then chocolate / everyone here knows how to cry / it's a long way down*)

And sometimes, I can't help myself.
I should be hung.

I kissed Dan the other day, and let him hold me, because I felt so alone. I had lost, in a process of a few days, not only the person I thought I was going to spend the rest of my life with, but also my best friend.

(*And if I shed a tear, I won't cage it, I won't fear love. I feel a rage, I won't deny it, I won't fear love.*)

I won't fear love.

I won't fear love.
I won't fear love.
I won't fear love.

(*Voices trapped in yearning, memories trapped in time / The night is my companion / Would I spend forever here and not be satisfied? / And I would be the one to hold you down / And kiss you so hard / I would take your breath away / And after I wipe your tears away just close your eyes dear / And through this world I've stumbled / so many times betrayed*)

You speak to me in riddles.
My body felt your breath.
You kept me alive.
Remember, that final night.

I could feel the weight of your skin next to me, so silky, and so smooth and I had died from sheer pleasure. And I remember that look on his face; I remember the way he looked at me when we were driving down the street; I had put my hand on his thigh and the way he blushed... I started giggling.

I remember when we met, and I could feel his heart beat so hard through his shirt.

I WON'T BE DENIED!
I WON'T BE DENIED!

And looking into his eyes, feeling his hand against my face and in this warped version of time, that moment, the way I see it, it's not from my perspective but from a third party's, as if they had stumbled upon us. And the look on his face, and the breathing, how intense, how ragged; just feeling him for the first time and standing up on tiptoe to kiss his chapped lips, to feel his hands on me and it felt so good.

Why did it have to end?
Why does one stop believing?

Why do I lie to myself and think, well, "Another one bites the dust," and it's like I carry on, with this brave face and manner everything is going to be okey dokey and it's like, in some way it's not. Not everything is going to be okay. It bothers the hell out of me about my past, I mean, 15 (+/-) guys in the past 22 months, is a FUCKING HELLUVA LOT. And if someone else told me that, I would think "Slut. Two bit trick."

I don't know what love is, but if it's anything like what I had with Michael.
I want it.
I crave it.

I don't want Dan to touch me, and he gets all upset when I refuse his advances. True, we are getting along better, I am **not** the easiest person to get along with, but, it's not Michael.

God, I'm fucked up.

Don, sometimes I feel grateful for him to push me as much as he does, probing things and making me see sides that I don't wanna see. I am ooh so tired right now and all I want to do is fall asleep wrapped in Michael's arms.

I fell hard.
And I am paying the price.

In many ways this is almost hysterical. Every guy I have spurned can be thinking, "Serves you right, you bitch." HA! You never had it so damn good.

My dear brother, Foosi and I were discussing me, naturally, every night since Michael and I broke apart, and one became two. And of course, dear Matt called me. They both said the same thing. "You're too much for these fools." Hell, Matt is the infamous Matt from *Downpour*, he should know, I mean, HE DID THE EXACT SAME THING A YEAR AGO! *Sigh*. Anywho, it is like, o'he of Michaelisms is following what his predecessors did before him and it makes me think even more.

It can't be the shoes!

So I think and I ponder and I cry out "WHY WHY WHY!" You know, why is it that all these guys keep telling me, "You're so special, I have felt your pain, come to Butthead," and I'm like "COOL!" and off I go?

I mean, its not like I'm out on the prowl, looking for these guys. They just fall in my lap.
And each is special in their own way.

My pattern is that I keep finding these guys who have been hurt by something or another and I pick them up, I help them, and I show them "HEY! This is what love is all about." They get weirded out on me and leave. And I am left questioning, "Why?"

WHY?

Foosi and I got into a **huge** fight last night when I started writing this. He told me that often in the last week he has wanted, very badly, to tell me, "Forget THEM. Let THEM have their lives and let US take our lives and make them one."

And I freaked.
I started attacking him, and saying all sorts of naughty things, I don't know.

He's been like the only constant thing in my life, and he emailed me last night and this morning, crying, and it was like, "I didn't give a shit." I started replying back and it's like, "Yeah, I am the girl that cried wolf," because when someone tells me what I want to hear, I freak out and start saying that it is lies and it is nothing more than a fucked attempt at living my life and nothing is real and nothing is really real. That is scaring me, because Foosi is **very** real, **very** real and he knows it and I know it too.

This whole damn thing smells to high heaven of unrequited love, you know, that "Ohh...I've been in love with you the whole time and it wasn't till now.." B-U-L-L-S-H-I-T.

I do **not** need this crap now, I mean, I just got dumped by Mr. Connection, poor Dan is tearing his heart apart, and nothing ever seems real to me, not anymore.

Thanks Don for the following song lyrics:

*Opiate* by tool

*Choices always were a problem for you / What you need is someone strong to guide you / Deaf and blind and dumb and born to follow / What you need is someone strong to use you like me/ Like me / If you want to get your soul to heaven / Trust in me / Don't judge or question / You are broken now / but faith can heal you / Just do everything I tell you to do / Deaf and blind and dumb and born to follow / Let me lay my holy hand upon you*

Yeah, damn.

I need to fly. I need to pack up my shit and go. I can't keep this up any longer. Searching, always searching for the holy grail, only to be let down, it's killing me. Killing me considerately, killing me kindly, yeah, yeah, yeah.

And it seems, that no matter how much you try, things just seem to get worse.

Today hanging out on #philosophy, we start debating about Marilyn Manson, and this guy pips up, "Marilyn is a person." I'm like, "Ummm yep, he sure is, I went out with him." And so this person starts messaging me, and I keep messaging him, "*Who are you?*" and I know, theoretically, who he is. He is the guy who wants Michael to run to Australia with him, and Michael wanted me to go (I guess, I dunno, that was then, this is now), but I wanted to know, and it's like, he kept saying things like, "I know things that you don't think I know…" and really weird stuff like that. And me, ohh Miss Imagination here, starts thinking *everything* and anything and then someone else later on saying they heard that I was a "porn star" in disguise. I'm like yeah well, *smirk*, I'm *not* but what the hell, might as well add it up to the days events right?

I mean, why is it so hard for people to stop the yelling and the screaming, the fear, the anxiety, the loneliness, the push/pull and just *be* themselves? Is that so hard to ask? Is that "so wrong?"

Yeah, I guess it is.

And so another 24 hr. rips by me, another day is done.

Thoughts.
Thoughts.
Thoughts.

Believe it or not, I actually did a spell check here, but there are some things that do not seem right, and heaven forbid that I do a grammar check, I mean, Microslut runs my life enough as it is, why should I let them have any more control?

I want it all.
I want a best friend.

I want someone I can tell my thoughts to, someone to share my dreams with, someone to be the object of my desires, someone to hold me when it rains, someone to laugh with, to giggle at, to make fun and tickle, someone I can read to when we are sleepy tired, to cook for and with, to go places with.

I want someone I can kiss in the middle of Mall of America.
Someone I can have and hold and think, "Yes..."
I want someone who will give me my freedom, but will keep me reined in when need be.

Someone who will argue with me.
Someone who will brush my hair.
Someone who is their own person, but isn't afraid of something, everything, anything, it.

And it seems that time keeps ticking, and I am getting older, and as I look upon my life, I do not see pain, and I do not see misery, but I see LIFE!

Glorious, glorious LIFE.

And it's like, I know that I have so much to give, that it's unreal, and yeah, I scare the bejesus out of them, but hell, I mean, it's *not* like I didn't warn them all beforehand, I mean, hell I have *DownPour* right?

And I have so much more.

But a part of me is screaming, it's too late, it's too late, it's too late. Time to bury the dead, sing a song, find a book, and forget, forget, forget.

And that is how I keep sane.

If it were not for my words, how the hell would I remember, hmmm.. how would I remember?

How can I forget? How can I forget the taste of one and the feel of another?

*(And now I'm realize / I'm living like a trucker / Even though I don't have the belly / Even though she followed me to California all the way / All I want to do is watch the telly)*

My sympathy has now turned to malice.

And it doesn't really matter anymore now does it?

Who where when there?

When I was a young girl, I always felt that I would meet Mr. Right (not Mr. Right Now) in a library, or a bookstore or a coffee shop. I will be reading or browsing, and I will see him. He will be tall, strong, and he will come over to me, and we will just look, and just *know*.

It's always been a school girl crush to feel that way about someone, to see, to know and think, this *is* the one.

"As you wish."

The stuff story books are made of. The once in a lifetime love.

Yeah, dreams, and fairies, and unicorns.

The loss of innocence, the return to that time when the world seemed so believable, and here I thought that I could save it all.

I mean, I guess that is my problem right?

I want to believe no matter what anyone says, and I am finding it harder and harder to do so.

No, what I am finding harder to believe is that there is **one** true person. Because how can I have connected with so many, only to be dropped, and reconnected and dropped and reconnected and dropped...

# ABOUT THE AUTHOR

Lisa Rabey was born in Toronto, Ontario, has lived across the US and travelled to many parts unknown and known. She currently lives near dragons with a high concentration of orcs.

When she was young, she used to want to write for Rolling Stone but ended up working anywhere and everywhere. She now shakes her cane at the whippersnappers on her lawn.

Lisa is a discriminating Guinness taster, ageing, alternative hipster, and eco-conscious. She is equally in love with Joy Division, Jane Austen, Doctor Who, reality and period television, and heaving bosom books. You can find her across the internets as @heroineinabook and at https://lisarabey.com,

Made in United States
North Haven, CT
22 September 2024

57343828R00036